A Stepping-Stone Book

LIGHT and SHADOW
BY
CAROL SCHWALBERG

Pictures by Lawrence Di Fiori

Parents' Magazine Press • New York

For Yvette Estevez

Text Copyright © 1972 by Carol Schwalberg
Illustrations Copyright © 1972 by Lawrence Di Fiori
All rights reserved
Printed in the United States of America

Library of Congress Cataloging in Publication Data
Schwalberg, Carol.
    Light and shadow.
    (A Stepping-stone book)
    SUMMARY: Examines the characteristics of light
and shadow.
    1. Light—Juvenile literature.   [1. Light.
2. Shades and shadows]   I. Di Fiori, Lawrence, illus.
II. Title.
PZ10.S378Li   535   74-174587
ISBN 0-8193-0538 (lib. bdg.)

Contents

One

A Time of Darkness

In the middle of the night the sky is nearly black. A little light comes from the moon and the stars, but not very much. The light is weak.

Go to the room where you sleep. Unless you take along a flashlight or turn on a light, it is hard to see the palm of your hand in front of your face. You cannot read this page, even though it is white.

You cannot see well at night because you need light to see. Night is the time of darkness.

Two

A Time of Light

As dawn breaks, light floods the room where you sleep. It is easy to see the palm of your hand. You can read this page, too. You have light to see.

The sun seems to hang low in the sky. A stream of light comes from the sun. At noon the sun will seem high in the sky. At the end of the day, the sun will be low in the sky. All day long, there will be enough light to read.

Day is the time of light.

Three

Where Light Comes From

You see during the day because of sunlight which comes from the sun 93 million miles away. (That distance is so great a plane would have to circle the globe 1,720 times to cover it.) The sun is a ball of burning gases. These gases burn so hot and so bright that sunlight can travel all the way to the earth. Sunlight comes from burning. We call a light that comes from burning a *hot* light.

Nature has other forms of light. During a summer storm, you may see lightning. Lightning is a flashing of electricity between clouds.

If you go to the country on a summer night, you may see the light that comes from fireflies. You may even see them in the park in the city.

(Some people call fireflies lightning bugs or glow worms.) Fireflies give off light when one chemical inside their bodies mixes with another chemical. Fireflies give off light, but no heat. We call a light without heat a *cold* light.

Some children catch the fireflies in large glass jars to see the light the fireflies give off. Then they set the fireflies free again.

Incandescent

Besides the light in nature, there are the lights people make. Have you looked at fires? Firelight comes from burning or heat. Have you noticed that when someone strikes a match, it gives off light? If the burning match touches a candle, the candle gives off light, too. If metal is heated until it becomes red-hot or white-hot, it gives off light, too. Are the fire, the match, the candle, and the heated metal hot lights or cold lights?

If you flick the switch on the wall, the electric bulb will glow. Inside the electric bulb is a metal wire. When you turn on the

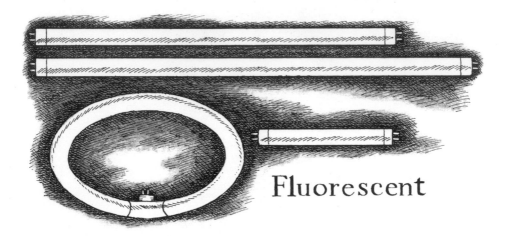

Fluorescent

electricity, the current makes the wire white-hot. It glows and gives off light. The light comes from heat. Some people turn off the lights to keep a room cool in summer.

We call the ordinary electric bulb an *incandescent* bulb. There are other types of electric bulbs.

One is the *fluorescent* bulb. Instead of a metal wire inside, this bulb has a special gas. When you turn on the electricity, the current makes the special gas give off a light you cannot see. This light you cannot see hits the special lining of the fluorescent bulb and makes it glow. We call the special material that glows fluorescent.

The fluorescent bulb sheds an even light, but makes little heat. Like the firefly, the fluorescent bulb gives off a cold light.

The fluorescent bulb, the electric bulb, the candle, the firefly, and the sun all give off light. We call something that gives off light a *luminous* object. Scientists say that luminous objects give off *energy*. They describe energy as the power to move things and to do work.

Since you are never going to see a beam of light push a wagon down the street, it is hard to think of light as energy. But you have already seen the energy of light at work. Light

helps camera film make pictures. Light helps plants grow. Light acts on our eyes and helps us see.

You can prove that light has energy. If you go outdoors on a sunny day and hold a magnifying glass over a piece of paper, the magnifying glass will focus light on one spot. In a short time the light will burn a hole there.

14

Here's another way to see light energy. Tear a brightly colored rag into two strips. Put one strip away in a drawer. Tape the other strip to a sunny wall. Look at both strips a week later. What has happened to the strip on the wall? It has lost some of its color, hasn't it? We call that loss of color fading. Light energy did that.

To prevent fading, people pull down the window shades or close the blinds to keep out the sunlight. For the same reason storekeepers sometimes put sheets of yellow plastic in their shop windows.

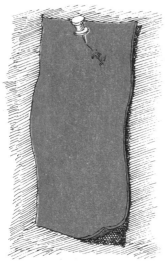

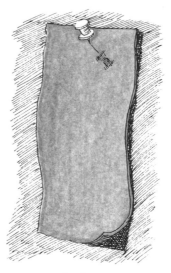

Before   After

Four

Brightness

Most electric bulbs you buy are marked in
watts and lumens. (If the marking is not on
the bulb, it will be on the carton.) Watts
measure the amount of electricity going into a
bulb. Lumens measure the amount of light a
bulb sheds, or the brightness it gives. The
more watts a bulb uses, the more power it
usually has to shed light. A 75-watt standard
bulb uses 75 watts of electricity. A 150-watt
standard bulb uses 150 watts.

The 150-watt bulb usually sheds twice as
much light as the 75-watt standard bulb. But if
you put a 75-watt bulb next to you and a
150-watt across the room, which bulb will shed

more light on your book? The closer you are to
the light, the more light you will receive, even
if the bulb near you is not so bright as the
other one.

Five

How Light Moves

At night when it's dark outside, turn on a flashlight. You will see that the beam of light moves in a straight line.

Since light moves in a straight line, you cannot see around a tree or a corner. That's why light helps you find things. Let's say that you are looking for a shoe under your bed. Since light moves in a straight line, the shoe is where it seems to be. If light turned around corners or bent in curves, you might not see your shoe. It would not be where you thought it was.

Six

Shadows

When light is blocked, you see a shadow. A shadow is the absence of light.

Every shadow must have light, something to block the light, and a flat surface for the shadow to fall on.

Do you know what things cast shadows? Stand up in the path of light. Do you cast a shadow? Hold a book up to the light. Does the book cast a shadow? Hold up a ball. Does it cast a shadow? You, the ball, and the book all cast shadows because you block the light. No light can come through you, the ball, or the book. We call anything no light can come through *opaque*.

Can light travel through a woolen blanket? A

piece of cardboard? A nylon stocking? Try it and see.

Not everything casts a shadow. Hold an empty glass to the light. Does it cast a shadow? Hold a glass filled with water to the light? Does it cast a shadow? An empty glass, a glass filled with water, and a nylon stocking do not cast shadows because they do not block the light. They let the light come through. When

something lets the light through and lets you see through it, we call it *transparent*.

If you hold a sheet of frosted glass to the light, does it cast a strong shadow? It lets light through, but you can't see through it. We call such material *translucent*.

If you stand with the sunlight behind you, where does the shadow fall? If you turn around and the light is in front of you, where does the shadow fall? A shadow always falls in the direction opposite the light.

If you hold your hands close to a flashlight or an electric bulb, does the shadow grow? If you take your hands away from the light, does the shadow shrink? (In sunlight, remember that the sun is overhead. The closer your hands are to the ground, the farther they are from the sun.) The closer something is to the light, the bigger its shadow will be.

Do shadows stay the same size all day long?
Go out to the playground, or the park, or your
backyard if you have one, and set a stick in the
earth or look for a low pole.

At nine in the morning, when the sun hangs
low in the sky, the light comes at an angle.
Is the shadow long? With a piece of chalk
mark the length of the shadow.

At noon, when the sun is overhead, the light comes straight down. Has the shadow moved? Is it shorter? Mark the length of the shadow again.

At three in the afternoon, when the sun has shifted again, has the shadow moved again? Is it longer? When light comes from an angle, the shadow will grow. The bigger the angle of the light, the longer a shadow will be.

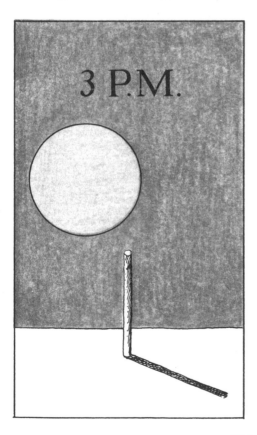

3 P.M.

You can use shadows to help you tell time. Stick a pencil into an empty spool of thread. Place them on a shelf or on a table where the sunlight can hit them. How does the shadow shift as the day goes by? If you mark off the length hour after hour, day after day, month after month, you will be able to tell time by the sun. You will have made a sun dial.

If you go into the schoolyard, the park, or the playground on a cloudy day, how does your shadow look? Is it paler than on a sunny day? Is there any shadow at all? The stronger the light, the stronger the shadow.

If you place a small toy on a table and shine a flashlight at it, is the shadow dark with sharp edges? If you slip a piece of tissue paper over the flashlight, does the shadow look dimmer? The weaker the light, the weaker the shadow will be.

If you hold the flashlight close to the toy, is the shadow black and strong? If you move the flashlight away, how does the shadow look? The farther away a light is, the weaker the shadow it makes.

Would you like to make two shadows with one toy? You will need two flashlights or two lamps without shades. If you keep both lights away from each other and turn them on at the same time, you will have two shadows. At

night, if you walk along a street with two
street lamps, one in front of you and one
behind you, you will cast two shadows yourself.

You can also play with shadows outdoors on a sunny day. If you would like to hide your own shadow, just walk into the shadow of a tree or a building.

As you move, does your shadow move too? You can catch your friend's shadow late in the day, when shadows are longest. If the friend jumps, what happens to the shadow? Can you catch it or not?

When you go into the playground or yard with your class, look at the shadows. Does your teacher's shadow look like her? Does your own shadow look like you? What about a car? Or a dog? The shape of a shadow follows the shape of the object that blocks the light.

You can use this fact to have fun at home or in school. Hang a sheet between two chairs, two stools, or two tables the same height. Set a strong light far behind the sheet. Have a group of friends walk in front of the light. Ask them to jump, hop, run. Can you tell one friend from another by their shadows?

33

Shadows can help you draw pictures. Tape a large piece of brown paper or newspaper to the wall. Take the shade off a lamp and turn the lamp on. Ask a friend to stand in front of the paper. Move the lamp and your friend until his profile casts a shadow on the paper. Trace

around the shadow with a crayon. Cut out this
portrait and you have a *silhouette*. Paste the
silhouette onto colored paper. Or trace around
the silhouette with chalk on black paper. Then
cut out the black silhouette and paste that
onto colored paper.

You can also use shadows to give plays. First think up a story. On big sheets of cardboard make an outline drawing of each character in the story. Cut out along the outline. Then ask someone strong to untwist the ends of wire hangers and straighten them out. Tape one hanger onto the center of each cardboard figure. Now tape a big sheet in a doorway. Turn on a light behind the sheet. Have one friend move each figure and say the words you have made up for that figure. People sitting in front of the sheet will see the figures move while they listen to the story. You will have your own theater!

Shadows can help you play tricks. You can use the light of a clear electric bulb to cast a strong shadow. To make the shadow of a duck, bend back all your fingers except the thumb and the first finger, which make the bill.

To make a rabbit, form a fist, then hold up the first and second fingers for the ears.

Seven

How Light Goes In

Light can travel into many things. Part or all of the light may stay there. When light stays inside an object, we say that the object *absorbs* light. (*Sorb* comes from a Latin word that means suck up or swallow.)

Dark objects take in more light than pale objects. How much light an object absorbs depends on how dark it is. Does a black shoe absorb a lot of light? How about an orange? Which absorbs more light?

If you have ever seen a room painted in a dark color and one painted white, you may have noticed that the white room seemed to have more light, even if both rooms had the same number of windows and lamps.

Eight

How Light Comes Back

All light doesn't go into an object. Some light bounces back. When the light comes back we say it is *reflected*. (*Flect* comes from the Latin word meaning to bend or turn.) What comes back we call the *reflection*.

Some things look very white. The whitest white reflects every bit of light that strikes it. If it reflects almost every bit of light, we still call it white. If it reflects half the light, it is gray. If it reflects no light at all, it is blackest black.

Can you see a white sheet in the dark? Light may travel in the dark, but we see light only when it is reflected by something. Everything we see comes from reflections.

You can see reflections in mirrors and lakes, puddles and ponds, hubcaps and metal spoons, glasses, and other people's eyes. Some materials, such as silver, aluminum, and stainless steel, reflect most of the light that strikes them.

When a reflection bothers you and makes it hard to see, we call it *glare*. If you take a magazine with shiny pages outside on a sunny

day, the shiny paper is hard to read. Can you read the same magazine on a cloudy day? Or in a room lighted by fluorescent bulbs? The light has to be very strong to create glare.

Each reflection needs light, something to be reflected, a smooth flat reflecting surface, and something dark behind the reflecting surface.

If you put a toy in front of the mirror and have someone turn off the light, there is no reflection. If you take the toy away from the mirror, the mirror won't reflect it.

If you look in a shop window when the shop is dark, you can see your reflection. What happens when the lights are turned on? If there is nothing to stop light from coming behind the reflecting surface, there is no reflection.

When a lake is calm and its surface smooth, you can see reflections as clearly as in a mirror. What happens on a stormy day? The wind whips up little waves, the surface is not smooth, and there is no reflection.

Have you ever looked at your face in a hubcap? Or in a metal spoon? If the reflecting surface is not flat, the reflection you see will be very funny, or distorted. Sometimes fairs and amusement parks have curved mirrors for people to look at and laugh. We call these fun-house mirrors.

You can make your own fun-house mirror. Borrow a shiny metal cookie sheet or pancake turner. Now bend it toward you. How do you look — bigger or smaller? In one spot or all over? Bend it slightly away from you. How do you look now?

If you stand in front of a real mirror and scratch your right cheek, does the person in the mirror scratch his right cheek? If you touch your left eyebrow, which eyebrow is touched in the mirror? A mirror never shows you how you look to others.

To see yourself as others see you, you need two mirrors. Hold the first mirror straight in front of you. Hold the second mirror next to the first mirror to form an L-shape. We call that L-shape a *right angle*. If you scratch your right cheek, does the person in the second mirror scratch his right cheek? If you touch your left eyebrow, do you see the left or the right eyebrow being touched?

You can also use a mirror to see around corners or over your head. Have other people ever blocked your view at a parade? Next time take along a mirror, turn your back to the crowd and hold the mirror high in front of you. Then you will see the parade. Light that hits a mirror bounces back at the same angle.

Periscope

Submarine commanders see over the tops of
their submarines by using a periscope. If you
want to make a periscope, take a milk carton,
two small pocket mirrors, and cellophane tape.
Cut one hole near the top on one side of the
carton and another hole on the opposite side
near the bottom. Tape mirrors in place, as they
are in the picture. Now look through the lower
hole. You will be able to see above you without
craning your neck.

47

Nine

How Light Seems to Bend

Light travels through space, air, water, and glass.

Light travels fastest through empty space because there is nothing to stop it. The rate through empty space is 186,282 miles per second. Light travels next fastest through air. The rate through air is 186,270 miles per second. That's like going around the earth more than eight times in one second. Try to imagine a ball bouncing 75 times a second. Light whizzes from New York City to Los Angeles in the time it takes for only the first two bounces.

Light travels more slowly through water than through air — at the rate of 139,000 miles per second. It travels still more slowly through glass — at the rate of 124,000 miles per second.

If a beam of light goes straight down into a glass of water, all parts of the light beam slow down at the same rate. You cannot see any change. If the beam of light enters the water at a slant, the light hitting the water first slows down first, but the rest keeps on moving at the same speed. The light seems to bend.

If you put a pencil in a glass of water, it will seem to be broken where it touches the water. When light seems to bend, we call it *refraction*. (*Fract* comes from the Latin word meaning to break.)

Refraction can play tricks with your eyes.
Crumple up a piece of aluminum foil and
smooth it out again. Fill a tall jar with water.
Set the jar on the foil. Does the foil under the
jar seem closer than the foil outside the jar?
Water makes things look closer than they are.
That's why it's hard to guess the depth of lakes
and swimming pools.

If you're ever in the country, pick two flowers of the same kind along the road. Or pick two dandelions in the park. Find two bottles — one curved and one with flat sides. Fill each bottle with water. Put one flower in the bottle with flat sides. Does the stem under water look thicker than the stem out of water? Water makes things seem larger than they are. Now put the second flower in the curved bottle. Does the second stem look thicker than the first stem? The curved bottle refracts the light more than the flat bottle.

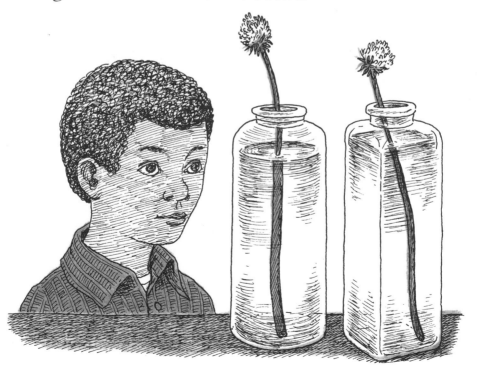

One kind of curved glass or plastic used to refract light is a *lens*. (*Lens* comes from the Latin word meaning lentil, the seed used in soup. The lentil has the same shape as a lens.)

One type of lens curves inward on both sides and is thicker at the edges than in the center. It is called *concave*. It bends light away from the center of the lens. A concave lens makes things look smaller than they are. If you are near-sighted, your glasses have concave lenses.

Another kind of lens curves outward and is thicker at the center than at the edges. It is called *convex*. It bends light toward the center of the lens. A convex lens makes things look larger than they are. (A magnifying glass is a convex lens.) If you are far-sighted, your glasses have convex lenses.

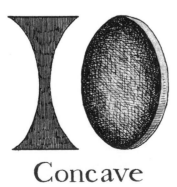

Concave

Convex

Ten

What Light Is

For hundreds of years scientists have wanted to know what light is. Now they have found not one but two answers.

In one answer, light is a package of energy bullets called *photons*. (*Photon* comes from a Greek word meaning light.) Photons are so tiny that billions could fit on the head of a pin.

The second answer is that light is a kind of wave, something like the waves of an ocean or the ripples caused by dropping a stone in calm water. The distance from the top of one wave to the top of another is a wave length. (See picture, page 54.) Light waves are so tiny that more than 100 could fit into the thickness of this page.

Light waves are only one of the big set of waves all around us. There are other waves for radio and television, heat and x-rays.

Scientists think of light as a package of photons when they try to capture its energy. They have turned the energy of sunlight into electricity by making a *solar cell*. (*Solar* comes from the Latin word meaning sun.) The solar cell is a thin, circular slice of one chemical plus tiny amounts of other chemicals. When sunlight falls on the circular slice, a tiny electric current flows. A group of solar cells forms a solar battery.

Solar batteries supply the electricity that makes voices louder along telephone lines. If the telephone line does not use all the electricity the battery makes on a sunny day, what is left goes into a storage battery. That storage battery will then feed electricity to the telephone line at night or on cloudy days.

Scientists have placed solar batteries on all

sides of the artificial satellites that go round the
earth. These batteries power the satellite's radio.
As the satellite turns, at least one battery
always faces the sun.

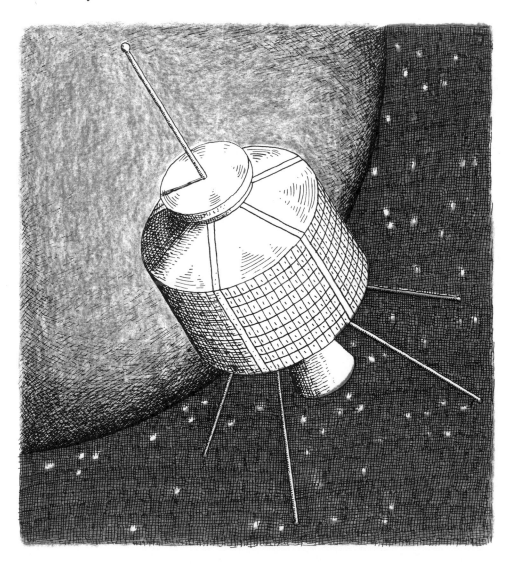

Eleven

Light and Color

Light seems to have no color at all, but the droplets of water in the air during a rainstorm change the speed of light and break it down into the colors of a rainbow. These are red, orange, yellow, green, blue, indigo, and violet.

If you want to make a rainbow, you'll need a garden hose. If you live in the city, you may be able to borrow one for a few minutes in the park, or at school. Late in the afternoon, stand with your back to the sun and spray water in front of you. Sunlight will pass through the water droplets and become a rainbow.

The colors of the rainbow make up the *spectrum*. Red is always at one end of the spectrum and violet at the other.
Each color in the spectrum has its own wave

length. Red has the longest wave length and violet the shortest wave length. These wave lengths are very tiny. If you could divide a line one inch long into 26,000 parts, each part would be bigger than the wave length of red light. Even so, that's more than twice the wave length of violet light.

Everything around you seems to have a color. The sky is blue. The grass is green. Why do you see colors that way?

The sky contains all colors of light, but it contains more blue rays than any other. As light passes through the air, it meets dust particles and tiny droplets of water. Some light is absorbed and turned into heat. The red light passes through, and the blue light is scattered.

When sunlight falls on grass, the grass absorbs the red and the blue waves of light, but reflects the green waves. Each object we see absorbs certain colors and reflects others. We see only the reflected colors.

Daylight contains all colors of the spectrum. In daylight a navy blue dress looks navy blue. Light from incandescent bulbs lacks some of the green and blue wave lengths. Under incandescent light a navy blue dress may absorb all the blue light that falls on it and look almost black. What color you see depends on the light you see it in. That's why many women, when shopping for a dress, will take it into the daylight to see the true color.

Twelve

The Light You Cannot See

Besides the light you can see, there is the light you cannot see. Next to red light on the spectrum are *infra-red* rays. They have an even longer wave length than red light. Next to violet light on the spectrum are *ultra-violet* rays. They have an even shorter wave length than violet light.

Infra-red carries most of the heating power of sunlight. Ultra-violet causes sunburn and fading. It also kills certain bacteria that cause diseases, and it helps the body make vitamin D, which helps your bones grow straight.

Black fluorescent bulbs give off a great deal of ultra-violet, but almost no light you can see. Anything white seen under black fluorescent light looks very bright and seems to glow, but everything else is nearly invisible.

Camera film that picks up infra-red light can take pictures in the dark. It can also take pictures in daylight. If you photograph a landscape, the leaves and the grass will look nearly white and the sky very dark. If you take a picture of a person, you will see veins in his face that you cannot ordinarily see.

The light you cannot see can change the way the things you *can* see look.

Light is a form of energy, and it performs many wonders. It gives us plants to eat and vitamin D for strong bones. Thanks to light, we can take pictures that last forever, and telephone friends who live miles away. Light gives us colors and reflections, the hush of night and the rush of day, and, best of all, the special joy of seeing.

Index